Golden Prayers

Golden Prayers

JO PETTY

Drawings by Martha Lindbo Heath

A DOUBLEDAY-GALILEE ORIGINAL

DOUBLEDAY & COMPANY, INC., GARDEN CITY, NEW YORK 1980

All wise thoughts have been thought already thousands of times, but to make them truly ours, we must think them over again honestly until they take place in our personal experience.

Library of Congress Cataloging in Publication Data

Petty, Jo.
Golden prayers.

"A Doubleday-Galilee original."
1. Prayers.   I. Title.
BV245.P43   242'.8
ISBN: 0-385-15364-3
Library of Congress Catalog Card Number 79–7505

CONTENTS

Golden Prayers

PREFACE

God is only a prayer away!

The secret of prayer is secret prayer!

Prayer is talking with God—the highest level we can attain!

Prayer is friendship with God!

In our life of prayer we need not travel an unmarked path. Jesus Himself is our teacher!

Our prayers are the way God chose to carry out His great work in the world!

We are a channel attached to unlimited divine resources!

The greatest thing we can do for God or man is pray!

We can do more than pray after we have prayed!

Nothing we can say about prayer is as profitable as praying!

Lord,
have mercy

Jesus calls us. By Your mercies
Savior, may we hear Your call,
Give our hearts to Your obedience,
Serve and love You best of all.

—Cecil Alexander, alt.

This we recall to mind, therefore have we hope. It is of Your mercy, Lord, that we are not consumed, because Your compassions fail not. They are new every morning. Great is Your faithfulness!

O praise the Lord, for Your merciful kindness is great toward us, and Your truth endures forever.

Not unto us, O Lord, not unto us, but unto Your Name we give glory, for Your mercy and for Your truth's sake.

You, O Lord, are full of compassion, and gracious, and plenteous in mercy and truth.

You, Lord, are good to all, and Your tender mercies are over all Your works.

Have we not all one Father? Has not one God created us? And You are no respecter of persons.

Let us therefore come boldly unto Your throne, that we may obtain mercy and grace that will help us in time of need.

Even when our father and our mother forsake us, You, Lord, will hold us up.

Hear, O Lord, and have mercy on us: be our helper always.

For a small moment You may have forsaken us, but with great mercies You will gather us.

If in wrath You hide Your face from us for a moment, with everlasting kindness have mercy upon us, our Lord and our Redeemer.

We ask You, Father: Will You cast us off forever? Will You be favorable no more? Is Your mercy gone forever? Have You forgotten to be gracious? Have You in anger shut up Your tender mercies? Help us, O Lord our God: save us according to Your mercy.

You, Lord, are good and ready to forgive, and plenteous in mercy unto all who call upon You.

To You, O Lord our God, belong mercies and forgiveness, though we have rebelled against You; neither have we obeyed Your voice to walk in Your laws.

Our smallest sin should humble us, but because of Your mercy we must not despair in our greatest sin.

Let Your mercies come to us, O Lord, even Your salvation, according to Your word.

Make Your face to shine upon us, save us for Your mercy's sake.

Look upon our affliction and our pain, and forgive all of our sins.

If we confess our sins, You are faithful and just to forgive our sins, and to cleanse us from all unrighteousness.

If we cover our sins, we shall not prosper, but if we confess and forsake them, we shall have Your mercy.

Have mercy upon us, O God, according to Your loving-kindness: according to the multitude of Your tender mercies, blot out our transgressions. Wash us thoroughly from our iniquities, and cleanse us from our sin, for we acknowledge our transgressions, and our sin is ever before us. Hide Your face from our sins, and blot out all our iniquities.

Create in us a clean heart, O God; and renew a right spirit within us.

Cast us not away from Your presence, and take not Your Holy Spirit from us.

Withhold not Your tender mercies from us, O Lord: let Your loving-kindness and Your truth continually preserve us. Innumerable evils have compassed us about; our iniquities have taken hold upon us, so that we are not able to look up; therefore our hearts fail us.

Broken spirits and contrite hearts, O God, You will not despise.

As we pray for forgiveness, Father, we forgive all who have offended us, for we know that You will not forgive us if we refuse to forgive anyone who has trespassed against us.

We forgive everyone every trespass, though it should reach seventy times seven times.

Restore unto us the joy of our salvation. Then shall we teach transgressors Your ways, and sinners shall be converted unto You.

Oh, satisfy us early with Your mercy, so that we may be glad and rejoice all of our days.

Your mercy, O Lord, is from everlasting to everlasting upon those who fear You.

We are now blessed, for our transgressions are forgiven and our sins are covered.

We have forgiven much because we love much.

17

Your mercy, O Lord, is on those who fear You from generation to generation.

And You have shown us what is good and what You require of us: to do justly, love mercy and walk humbly with You.

Blessed are the merciful, for they shall obtain mercy.

Not by works of righteousness that we have done, but according to Your mercy You have saved us, by the washing of regeneration, and the renewing of the Holy Spirit which You shed on us abundantly through Jesus Christ, our Savior.

May we always show mercy with cheerfulness.

All Your paths, Lord, are mercy and truth to such as keep Your covenant and Your testimonies.

We trusted in Your mercy, Lord, and our hearts rejoice in Your salvation.

We will sing unto You, for You have dealt bountifully with us.

Unto You, O our Strength, will we sing: for You are our defense, and the God of our mercy.

We will be glad and rejoice in Your mercy, for You have considered our trouble; You have known our souls in adversities.

The earth, O Lord, is full of Your mercy; teach us Your statutes.

Show us Your ways, O Lord; teach us Your paths.

Mercy and truth are met together; righteousness and peace have kissed each other.

Ever give us that wisdom from above which is first pure, then peaceable, gentle and easy to be entreated, full of mercy and good fruits, without partiality, and without hypocrisy, which You have promised to give liberally to all that ask You.

You shall hide us in the secret of Your presence from the pride of man; You shall keep us secretly from the strife of tongues. We bless You, Lord, for You have shown us Your marvelous kindness.

May we keep ourselves in Your love, looking for the mercy of our Lord Jesus Christ unto eternal life.

As the called of You, our God, holy and beloved, may our hearts be filled with mercies, kindness, humility, meekness; may we forbear one another and forgive one another, even as Christ forgave us.

Give us thankful hearts for all Your mercies. There is a wideness in Your mercy like the wideness of the sea!

O God, Whose mercies cannot be numbered, we will sing of Your power; yea, we will sing aloud of Your mercy in the morning, for You have been our defense and refuge in the day of our trouble.

We bless You, O God, for You have not turned away our prayers.

You have not dealt with us after our sins, nor rewarded us according to our iniquities. As the heaven is high above the earth, so great is Your mercy toward those who fear You.

With You, Lord, there is mercy, and with You is plenteous redemption. We thank You for forgiving the sins of all who are penitent.

When we think upon all Your mercies, Father, we are lost in wonder, love and praise!

We bless You, our Lord, and forget not all Your benefits: You forgive all our iniquities, You heal all our diseases, You redeem our life from destruction. You crown us with loving-kindness and tender mercies, You satisfy our mouth with good things, so that our youth is renewed like the eagle's!

O Lord, Your tender mercies and Your loving-kindness have been from the beginning!

Surely goodness and mercy shall follow us all the days of our lives, and we shall dwell in Your house forever.

'Lord,
teach us love'

Father, lead us in the more excellent way—Love.

When Faith has said, "Father," then Love steps in and says, "Our Father—give us."

The simple heart that freely asks in love, receives.

May we love enough to pray.

He prays best who loves best.

Our Father in heaven,
What wondrous love is this? You gave Your only begotten Son, so that whosoever believes in Him should not perish, but have everlasting life!

Thanks be unto You for Your unspeakable gift!

Father, You made Jesus, Who knew no sin, to be sin for us, that we might be made the righteousness of God in Him.

Father, forgive our lack of love. Even when we have loved, we have not loved fervently.

Our love is weak—we love only those who love us. We speak only to those who speak to us.

Forgive us, Lord, for we have never loved anybody but ourselves enough—not even our families and friends. How could we love our enemies?

We are so slow to forgive, but we want You to forgive us instantly. May we learn to forgive quickly as little children do.

If we love even one, we find that we love that person more than we love You, and then we are not worthy of You. Forgive.

We have not loved the stranger. Forgive.

So fill us with Your love that we may do nothing that displeases You.

> Love is kind and suffers long,
> Love is meek and thinks no wrong,
> Love than death itself more strong;
> Therefore, give us love.
> —Christopher Wordsworth, alt.

Oh, give us brother-love, so that we may more clearly see the Word made flesh and in a manger laid.

Father, Who has made of one blood all nations of men to dwell on the face of the earth, help us to live as brothers.

Turn the hearts of the parents to the children and the hearts of the children to the parents.

Give us this day our daily bread, which includes love, joy and peace, which can come only from You, our Father.

Increase in us true religion.

Each day may we remember that every good gift and every perfect gift is from You, Father.

Give us the will to honor You with our substance and the first fruits of all our increase.

May we have a continual sense of Your abiding Presence.

May no clouds of our mortal life hide the light of Your love from us.

Help us to tell others of Your love.

Give us grace to help all we know who are in need.

May we love all who are living in mental darkness.

Make us quick to see the needs of those less fortunate than ourselves.

Remind us that every deed of love we do to another is done to You, Father.

Cause Your light to shine in our hearts so that others may see The Way.

Give us a desire to do all things for love of You.

May we so love You that we may give love to others.

Give us grace to love You with all our heart and soul and mind and strength.

Give us grace to love our neighbors as ourselves.

> Lord, it is our chief complaint
> That our love is weak and faint;
> Yet we love You and adore;
> O for grace to love You more.
> —William Cowper, alt.

Help us to love, to serve one another, and in honor to prefer one another.

Keep us ever mindful of the needs of others.

May our love abound more and more.

May we without ceasing remember others in our prayers night and day.

Teach us that our prayers can bring blessings to others.

Teach us that love covers all sins.

Deepen our affections.

May we set our affections on things above rather than on things on the earth, keeping in mind that the things that are seen are temporal and the things that are not seen are eternal.

May we always have care one for another, knowing that as when one member of our body suffers, all of the members suffer with it, so it is with the members of the body of Christ: when one member suffers, all of the members suffer. Give us Your love, which will make us care one for another.

Enrich our homes with the simple joy that comes from loving one another.

As You are the Father of us all, so let us live as members of one family.

Never let us forget the poor, or those sick or in prison or hungry or thirsty, for inasmuch as we do it not to them, we do it not to You, dear Lord.

We bless You for the love of friends in heaven and in earth.

> Dear Jesus,
> May we know You more clearly,
> May we love You more dearly,
> May we follow You more nearly.

Help us to live this day in love of You and in obedience to Your holy will.

May we daily become more and more like Jesus.

May we try to understand rather than seek to be understood.

Give us the power to forgive all who have trespassed against us, so that we may be forgiven our trespasses against You.

Forgive us our sins, for we also forgive every person who is indebted to us.

Lay not this sin to their charge.

Father, forgive them, for they know not what they do.

Jesus taught us that if we forgive those who trespass against us, You, Father, will forgive our trespasses.

We know it is in Christ that we have redemption through His blood, the forgiveness of sins according to His grace.

We understand that though our sins be as scarlet, they shall be white as snow; though they be red like crimson, they shall be as wool.

We have forsaken our ways and unrighteous thoughts, Lord, and have returned to You and You have abundantly pardoned.

We acknowledged our sins unto You and our iniquities have we not hid. We confessed our transgressions unto You and You forgave the iniquity of our sins.

May we now walk in the light as You are in the light, that we may have fellowship one with another, and that the blood of Jesus Christ, Your Son, our Lord, will continually cleanse us from all sin.

Thank You, Father, for forgiving our sins, for the wages of sin is death; but Your gift is eternal life through Jesus Christ, our Lord.

Thank You, Father, for the knowledge that we have passed from death unto life because we love our brothers.

Father, we thank You for the comfort received from the Holy Spirit's bringing to our remembrance that Jesus lives and is ever interceding for us.

Since Christ pleased not Himself, may we please our neighbors rather than ourselves.

Increase our love, O Lord, so that our spirit of forgiveness will increase.

Help us to love those who do not love us and to be good to those who are not good to us.

Help us to love our enemies.

Help us to give without counting the cost.

Help us to labor without asking for any reward.

Since the love of money is the root of all evil, may we not love silver and gold, which will not satisfy.

We are grateful for our material possessions. May we not set our hearts upon them.

Thank You for giving us eternal life; we shall never perish, neither shall any man pluck us out of Your Hand. We are fully persuaded that neither death, nor life, nor angels, nor principalities, nor powers, nor things present, nor things to come, nor height, nor depth, nor any other creature shall be able to separate us from the love of God which is in Christ Jesus, our Lord.

Your love, O God, and Your blessings have ever been of old, but are now, and here and everywhere!

Your greatness is revealed everywhere. The microscope and the telescope reveal You, and no one can fail to see that the heavens declare Your glory and the firmament shows Your handiwork.

We also pray when we can only stand and wonder at Your greatness and goodness! It is an act of worship to rise above our needs and pains and say, How excellent is Your Name in all the earth. My God, how great You are!

Thank You, Father, for making it simple enough for us to understand that we should believe in the Name of Your Son, Jesus Christ, and love one another.

May we never forget that You have not redeemed us with silver and gold, but with the precious blood of Christ!

Thank You for Your love, which is shed abroad in our hearts by the Holy Spirit, Who is given unto us.

Thank You, Father, for giving us not the spirit of fear, but of power and of love and of a sound mind.

Thank You for supplying all of our needs according to Your riches in Christ Jesus.

Thank You for the angels that You send to minister for us who shall be heirs of salvation.

Father, we remember that You note the sparrow's fall and that the very hairs of our head are numbered. You know our every need and You desire nothing but good for us.

Since You spared not Your Own Son, but delivered Him up for us all, we know that You with Him will freely give us all things.

> We look to You in every need
> And never look in vain.
> We feel Your strong and tender love
> And all is well again.
> —Samuel Longfellow, alt.

Thank You for Your love. You pity us as a father pities his children. You know our frame. You remember that we are dust.

Lord,
give us joy

A Christian's daily business is prayer.

Earnest prayer is a way of life.

Prayer is practicing the presence of God.

Prayer is the soul's purest joy.

Blessed is the person You choose, Father, and cause to approach unto You.

Lord of all joy,
Unto Whom all hearts are open, all desires known,
May we declare Your works with rejoicing.

We praise You from Whom all blessings flow!

Many, O Lord our God, are Your wonderful works that You have done. They cannot be reckoned up in order unto You: if we would declare and speak them, they are more than can be numbered.

You cause the grass to grow for the cattle, and herbs for the service of man, that we may bring forth food out of the earth, and wine which makes glad our hearts, and oil to make our faces shine, and bread which strengthens our hearts!

O Lord, how manifold are Your works! In wisdom have You made them all; the earth is full of Your riches.

Help us to make known to the sons of men Your mighty acts and the glorious majesty of Your kingdom.

May we always abound in Your work, for we know our labor in You is not in vain.

Bless all who work with their hands, so that they may labor for Your honor.

Make us glad to help in Your work, so that all people everywhere may learn Your love and share the joy that comes through our Savior, Jesus Christ.

Help us to be faithful in the discharge of our duties this day.

Help us to put away all selfish ambition.

Help us to do today's work well.

Give us a fervent spirit so that whatsoever we do, we do it heart-ily as unto You, Lord.

May we never be deaf to Your voice or blind to Your light.

And since it is through much tribulation that we enter into the kingdom, may we rejoice in all our sufferings which You allow.

May we be joyful when we are persecuted for righteousness' sake, for ours is the kingdom of heaven.

Happy are they who mourn, for they shall be comforted.

May we meet the anxieties and trials of our lives with constant cheerfulness.

May we glory in our infirmities, that Your power may rest upon us.

May we be happy, may we be glad, for the joy that comes from You, Lord, is our strength.

May we never forget to turn to You in all of our grief.

May we share our neighbors' sorrows as well as their joys.

If we seek You, Father, we shall not lack any good thing.

> When comforts are declining,
> God grant our souls again
> A season of clear shining,
> To cheer us after rain.
> —William Cowper, alt.

Unless Your law had been our delight, we would have perished in our afflictions.

Grant us Your peace and the joy of Your love.

May we pass this day in gladness.

We sing unto You and give thanks, for Your anger endures but a moment; in Your favor is life: weeping may endure for a night, but joy comes in the morning.

You are our strength and our shield. Our hearts trust in You, and we are helped; therefore, we greatly rejoice, and praise You in singing.

We rejoice in the knowledge of Your love through Jesus Christ, our Lord.

You are our strength and our song, and are become our salvation.

Happy is the man to whom You, Lord, impute not iniquity, and in whose spirit there is no guile.

Your tender, righteous, joyous will be done!

May we in everything give thanks, for this is the will of God in Christ Jesus concerning us.

It is a good thing to give thanks unto You, Lord.

May we give thanks always for all things unto God the Father in the Name of our Lord Jesus Christ, speaking to ourselves in psalms and hymns and spiritual songs, singing and making melody in our hearts to You, Lord.

Thank You for removing our transgressions from us as far as the east is from the west.

Thank You for giving us the desires of our hearts.

Thank You for never leaving us, never forsaking us.

Thank You for giving us even more than we pray for.

Thank You for this day in which to rejoice and be glad.

Thank You for the joy that You have put in our hearts.

Lord, You have done great things for us, whereof we are glad.

Thank You for teaching us that it is more blessed to give than to receive.

Thank You for giving us richly all things to enjoy.

Thank You for the Bible, which You gave so that our joy might be full.

Give us true freedom, which is through Jesus, for if the Son makes us free, we are indeed free.

May we give and give cheerfully, for You, Father, love a cheerful giver.

Give us grace so that, whether we eat or drink or whatsoever we do, we do it to Your glory.

Father, from Whom alone comes all true joy, keep our hearts fixed on You.

May we think on praise. May we think on things lovely, pure, true, honest, virtuous—on Your good news.

May all good learning abound and flourish.

Write Your law in our hearts, Father; then shall we delight to do Your will.

May our work and our recreation be one with the spirit in which we pray.

Open our eyes to the beauty all around us.

You make the outgoings of the morning and evening to rejoice.

You are blessed, O Lord God of our fathers: You are praised and exalted above all forever.

Holy, Holy, Holy, Lord God of hosts, heaven and earth are full of Your glory: Glory be to You, O Lord most high.

We praise You, O God; we acknowledge You to be the Lord, and we hallow Your Name.

We praise You, O God, for giving us the light of the knowledge of Your glory in the face of Jesus Christ.

You are the Lord and greatly to be praised!

Blessing, and glory, and wisdom, and thanksgiving, and honor, and power, and might, be unto You, our God forever and ever!

We will rejoice in You, Lord, the Righteous, and give thanks at the remembrance of Your holiness.

You reign, O Lord; let the earth rejoice!

You are the King of all the earth. You are the Lord, and there is none else. There is no God but You, our Lord.

The sea is Yours, and You made it; and Your hands formed the dry land.

The day is Yours, the night also is Yours; You have prepared the light and the sun; You have set all the borders of the earth; You have made summer and winter.

Father, it is Your good pleasure to give us the kingdom.

> No eye has seen, no ear has heard,
> Nor sense, nor reason known
> What joys You, Father, have prepared
> For those who love Your Son!
>
> —Isaac Watts, alt.

Lord, give us peace

The secret of peace: the constant referral of all anxieties to God.

None but God can satisfy the longings of the immortal soul.

> Are you weary? Are you troubled?
> Are you sore distressed?
> Come to Jesus, and in coming
> Be at rest.
>
> —John Mason Neale, alt.

Father, we have proven over and over that we need more than bread. Earthly things do not satisfy us. Give us the bread of life so that our souls may truly live.

There is a want in our hearts that all creation can never supply.

Our Father in heaven, God of all comfort, Lord of all calm,

> O what peace we often forfeit,
> O what needless pain we bear—
> All because we do not carry
> Everything to You in prayer.
> —Joseph Scriven, alt.

You practically beg us to pray, Father. You tell us to ask—seek—knock. You promise us that if we abide in You and Your words abide in us, we may ask what we will and it shall be done unto us.

May we hearken to Your commandments, so that our peace may be as a river and our righteousness as the waves of the sea.

May our hearts keep Your commandments (love You and love our neighbor as ourselves), for long life and peace shall be given us.

Great peace have all who love Your law.

May we in everything, by prayer and supplication, with thanksgiving, being careful for nothing, let our requests be made known unto You, Father, Who know our needs before we ask; then Your peace, which passes all understanding (and all misunderstanding), shall keep our hearts and minds through Christ Jesus.

Jesus, You told us to let not our hearts be troubled, and not to be afraid. You promised to give us Your peace, which is not the peace the world gives.

Give us Your peace, Father, and our hearts shall not be troubled and we shall have no fear.

Father in heaven, we confess that we have sinned against You in thought, word and deed. Have mercy upon us after Your great goodness; according to the multitude of Your mercies, cleanse us from our sins, for Jesus' sake.

And, Lord, we have sinned against our neighbor, and therefore against You. May we not delay to seek reconciliation with our neighbor as Jesus taught us.

Give us the Holy Comforter, Father.

> Return, O holy Dove, return
> Sweet messenger of rest;
> We hate the sins that made You mourn
> And drove You from our breast.
> —William Cowper, alt.

Pardon our iniquities so that You may not withhold good things from us.

Father, You know our sorrows—comfort us in our loss and loneliness.

Deliver us from despair and self-pity.

O God, keep us peaceful through all trouble, forgiving and forgiven.

Glory be to You, Who loves us and has loosed us from our chains of sin.

We fear no evil, for we constantly give ourselves into Your keeping.

May Your peace, O Lord, forever rule in our hearts.

Thank You, Father, for making the storm a calm so that the waves are stilled.

Glory be to You in heaven, and on earth, peace and goodwill toward men.

May we pass this day in peace.

As You abide in us and we abide in You, we are free from fear and are filled with quietness and confidence.

May we fear nothing but the loss of You.

Thank You for giving us peace, even in tribulation.

Be the guardian of our daily lives.

Teach us to try to live peaceably with all persons.

Help us to be of one accord and of one mind.

May we endeavor to find the unity of Your Spirit in the bond of peace.

Give us the Holy Comforter, Who is the Holy Spirit, to teach us all things, to lead us into all truth.

We want the Holy Spirit, Who will search our hearts and make intercession for us according to Your will, Father.

Unite us all in You, as You, O Father, with Your Son and the Holy Spirit, are one God.

> The Spirit's gentle voice may we hear,
> Soft as the breath of even,
> That checks each fault, that calms each fear,
> And speaks of heaven.
>
> —Harriet Auber, alt.

May we be still and know that You are God!

Grant us Your peace in all our sorrows.

We bless You, Father of our Lord Jesus Christ, the Father of mercies, and the God of all comfort, Who comforts us in all our tribulation, that we may be able to comfort those who are in any trouble, by the comfort wherewith we ourselves are comforted of You, O God.

We will not fear, neither will we be dismayed, for You are our God: You will strengthen us. Yes, You will keep us; yes, You will uphold us with the right hand of Your righteousness.

Be with us and we shall fear no evil, for Your rod and Your staff comfort us, even though we walk through the valley of the shadow of death.

We will lay us down in peace and sleep, for You, Lord, only make us to dwell in safety.

May we be content, for we have food and clothing.

Thank You for teaching us that we live not unto ourselves, but if we live, we live unto the Lord, and if we die, we die unto the Lord; if we live, therefore, or die, we are the Lord's. For Jesus revived that He might be Lord of both the dead and the living. To live is Christ and to die is gain. Because He lives we shall live also.

Except You build our house, Lord, we work in vain.

Except You keep our city, Lord, the watchmen wake in vain.

The horse is prepared for battle, but our safety comes from You.

May we learn meekness; then shall we delight ourselves in the abundance of peace.

Your kingdom is not meat and drink, but righteousness, and peace, and joy in the Holy Spirit.

God of hope, fill us with all joy and peace in believing, that we may abound in hope through the power of the Holy Spirit.

Being justified by faith, we have peace with You, Father, through our Lord, Jesus Christ.

You, Father, are not the author of confusion, but of peace.

May we seek peace and pursue it.

Father, You only are our rock and our salvation; You are our defense: we shall not be greatly moved.

In troubled times we will call upon You, and You will answer us.

Father, should Your mercy send us
Sorrow, toil and woe,
Or should pain attend us
On our path below,
Grant that we may never
Fail Your hand to see;
Grant that we may ever
Cast our care on Thee.
—James Montgomery, alt.

You are our refuge and strength, a very present help in trouble. Therefore will we not fear though the earth be removed and though the mountains be carried in the midst of the sea. You are our hiding place; You shall preserve us from trouble; You shall compass us about with songs of deliverance.

How peacefully may we commit ourselves to the hand of Him Who bears up the world!

We pray for all in authority, so that we may lead a quiet and peaceable life, in all godliness and honesty.

May our ways please You, Lord, for then You make even our enemies to be at peace with us.

Fountain of all wisdom, give us wisdom, for her ways are pleasantness and her paths are peace.

Give us the fear of You, which is the beginning of wisdom, so that we may abide satisfied and not be visited with evil.

Give us wisdom and understanding, which is greater than all the riches of the world.

Give us wisdom, for it is better than rubies and diamonds, better than silver and gold—even choice silver and fine gold.

Give us wisdom so that we may dwell safely and be quiet from fear of evil.

Be our refuge, Lord, and our castle, O Most High, and no evil shall befall us, neither shall any plague come near our dwelling, for You shall give Your angels charge over us, to keep us in all our ways.

When we call upon You, You will answer. You will be with us in trouble; You will deliver us, and honor us.

You will satisfy us with long life and show us Your salvation.

And You give us, Your beloved, sleep! Thanks.

Your Word, O Lord, is a lamp unto our feet and a light unto our path. Your Word provides satisfactory answers to all of our problems. From the Bible we receive comfort and hope.

If we will draw near to You, You will draw near to us.

May we learn to forget those things that are behind, and reach forth unto those things that are before, and press toward the mark for the prize of Your high calling in Christ Jesus.

May we follow after the things which make for peace, and things wherewith one may edify another.

You, Lord, have promised to keep us in perfect peace if our minds are stayed on You, because we trust in You.

Eternal God, You are our refuge and underneath are Your everlasting arms.

If we seek You, Lord, You hear us and will deliver us from all our fears.

In the multitude of our thoughts within us, Your comforts delight our souls.

Father, bless us and keep us. Make Your face to shine upon us and be gracious unto us. Lift up Your countenance upon us, and give us peace.

Lord,
teach us patience

Patience is the art of hoping.

Patience is the greatest and sublimest power.

Doing God's will often means patiently waiting.

Wounds heal gradually.

Patience lies at the root of both pleasure and power.

Patience is hoping, waiting, watching, praying.

Patience is the very soul of peace.

Patience is genius.

O God of patience and consolation,
We praise You for Your goodness and mercy, which shall follow us all the days of our lives, and for the hope that we shall dwell with You forever.

Help us to lay aside every weight, and the sin that does so easily beset us; may we run with patience this race of life.

Grant that we may run a straight race and not be weary.

Give us the power of patience. When we are weak, with patience we can become strong. When strong, without patience we can become very, very weak.

Give us patience with one another.

May we daily be patient in little annoyances. Then, when threatened by a great temptation, we can escape by the door of patience.

Teach us to daily bear and forbear.

Teach us to bear our infirmities with cheerful patience.

Help us to hang in there, Lord. May we hold on, hold fast, for Your delays are never denials.

You are so patient with us, Lord. Help us to be patient with others and patient with ourselves.

You love us, Lord, yet you chasten us and scourge every child You receive.

If we endure chastening, You deal with us as with Your children.

No chastening, for the present, seems to be joyous, but grievous; nevertheless, afterward it yields the peaceable fruit of righteousness.

O patient God, our Father, rebuke us not in Your wrath; neither chasten us in Your displeasure.

Correct us, O Lord, not in Your anger, but with judgment, lest You bring us to nothing.

If You put us through the consuming fire, You will be in the furnace with us.

We pray not to be carried to the skies on satin beds of ease while others must fight to win the prize or must sail through bloody seas.

May we not despise Your chastening nor be weary of Your correction, for You are dealing with us as a father deals with the child in whom he delights.

A bruised reed You will not break, O God.

Father, You uphold all that fall and raise up all that be bowed down.

Though we walk in the midst of trouble, You will revive us.

Let us return unto You, Lord, for You have torn and You will heal us, You have smitten and You will bind up.

We know, O Lord, that Your judgments are right, and that You in faithfulness have afflicted us.

It is good for us that we have been afflicted, that we might learn Your statutes.

Be merciful unto us, O God, be merciful unto us, for we trust in You: in the shadow of Your wings will we make our refuge until these calamities be overpast.

We faint for Your salvation, but we hope in Your Word.

If we hope for that which we see not, then do we with patience wait for it, Father.

If we wait on You, and are of good courage, You have promised to strengthen our hearts.

May we ever rejoice in hope, be patient in tribulation, and continue instant in prayer.

O Lord, only You are our help. Make haste unto us, O God. You only are our deliverer. Do not delay, dear Lord.

Forgive us for not seeing with our eyes, or hearing with our ears, or understanding with our hearts.

Forgive us for calling You Lord when we are disobeying You.

Save us, O God, for the waters are come in unto our souls. We sink in deep mire, where there is no standing. We are come into deep waters where the floods overflow us. We are weary of our crying; our throats are dried; our eyes fail while we wait for You.

Save us, O Lord, for Your Name's sake; for Your righteousness' sake bring us out of trouble.

Give us help from trouble, for vain is the help of man.

We wait for You, Lord, for You are our help and our shield. Our hearts shall rejoice because we trust in Your holy Name.

Let us not be weary in well doing: for in due season we shall reap, if we faint not.

We will hope continually, and will yet praise You more and more.

May we not be unwise. May we understand what Your will is, O Lord.

Teach us to do Your will, for You are our God.

Your will is to draw all men together as one family in Christ. We pray that Your will be done.

Your will is that there be one fold and one shepherd. May this also be our will.

We know the world passes away, and the lust thereof: May we do Your will and abide forever.

Your will be done, which is to have all men be saved and come to a knowledge of the truth.

Stir our wills to pray and to work until Your will is done in earth, as it is in heaven.

May we spend freely and be spent for the salvation of others.

May we with lively faith labor abundantly to make known Your love in the gift of eternal life through Jesus Christ, our Lord.

Order our days according to Your divine will.

May we labor fervently in prayers so that we may stand perfect and complete in all Your will, O Father.

It is not Your will, Father, that one of these little ones should perish.

May we be not conformed to this world, but transformed by the renewing of our minds, so that we may prove what is that good, and acceptable, and perfect will of You, our God.

We wait for You, Lord, and in Your Word do we hope.

All Your waves and Your billows are gone over us.

Let us search and try our ways, and turn again to You, Lord. Help us to seek You with our whole heart so that we may find You.

Our times are in Your Hand!

Father, if this cup may not pass away from us unless we drink it, Your will be done.

We praise you in tribulations also, knowing that tribulation works patience; and patience, experience; and experience, hope.

Father, we wait upon You; our expectation is from You.

You tell us that a just man falls seven times and rises up again. May You never let go our hand when we stumble.

Grant us Your help in all of our troubles.

Grant us Your protection in all danger.

Give us patience, which we need so that after we have done Your will we may receive the promise. Our help and shield, we wait for You.

May we patiently endure so that we may obtain the promise.

We are willing to suffer, O Lord, if it be Your will, and we commit our souls unto You. Deliver us from needless suffering.

May our suffering teach us sympathy.

It is good that we should both hope and quietly wait for Your salvation, which hope we have as an anchor of the soul, both sure and steadfast.

God of all grace, Who has called us unto Your eternal glory by Christ Jesus, after we have suffered awhile, make us perfect, establish us, strengthen us.

We praise you because our light affliction, which is but for a moment, will work for us a far more exceeding eternal weight of glory.

May we prove all things and hold fast that which is good.

Give us strength, O Christ, and we can do all things.

Help us to walk in the way that we would have our children walk, dear Lord.

Make us aware that we suffer more from our grief and anger than from the things that grieve and anger us.

Father, we thank You for all the discipline in life, for the tasks and trials that teach us patience.

We will call upon You in the day of our trouble and You will deliver us and we will glorify You.

We have waited patiently for You, O Lord, and You inclined unto us and heard our cry. You brought us up also out of a horrible pit, out of the miry clay, and set our feet upon a rock, and established our goings. And You have put a new song in our mouths: Your praises.

Father, we thank You that You have heard us.

Thank You for the promise that all things work together for good to those who love You. We reckon that the sufferings of this present time are not worthy to be compared with the glory that shall be revealed in us. Many are the afflictions of the righteous; but You, O Lord, will deliver us out of them all, for which we thank You.

Your grace is sufficient for us; Your strength is made perfect in weakness. Gladly, therefore, will we rather glory in our infirmities so that the power of Christ may rest upon us. Therefore we take pleasure in infirmities, in reproaches, in necessities, in persecutions, in distresses for Christ's sake: for when we are weak, then are we strong.

Our strength is in waiting.

We ought always to pray and not to faint.

May we wait on You, our God, continually.

Make us patient in hard times, thoughtful in good times, and give us faith for the future.

Father, You gave us the Bible for our learning, so that we, through the patience and comfort of the scriptures, might have hope.

How rich we are if we have patience. How poor we are if we don't.

Give us patience to wait upon You, Lord, Who shall renew our strength: we shall mount up with wings as eagles; we shall run and not be weary; and we shall walk, and not faint.

Give us understanding, so that we may be able to withstand.

May we ask You for all we need and then, while waiting, work for all we ask.

Give us daily bread to fill our hungry body and soul.

With You as our constant friend, Lord, we can overcome the trials and temptations of this day.

Keep us faithful unto death so that we may receive the crown of life.

Help us to endure to the end, and we shall be saved.

Strengthen us with all might, according to Your glorious power, unto all patience with joyfulness.

Sometimes, Lord, You wait so that You may be gracious unto us. We are blessed if we wait for You.

Father, let patience have her perfect work, that we may be perfect and entire, wanting nothing.

Lord,
teach us goodness

We do the most good by being good.

Goodness is love in action.

As we pray, in like manner should we live.

Beauty is the mark God gives to virtue. Those who are good are always beautiful.

The prayer of the upright is God's delight.

Prayer is not eloquence, but earnestness.

God will bless a righteous man; with favor will He compass him as with a shield.

The earth is full of the goodness of You, our God!

Oh, how great is Your goodness, which You have laid up for those who fear You, which You have wrought for those who trust in You before the sons of men.

> Full of kindness and compassion,
> Slow to anger, vast in love,
> You are good to all creation;
> All Your works Your goodness prove.
> —Richard Mant, alt.

And Your goodness endures continually!

You have promised that while the earth remains, seedtime and harvest, cold and heat, summer and winter, and day and night shall not cease.

> Through every month Your gifts appear,
> Great God, Your goodness crowns the year!
> —Isaac Watts

Thank You for Your goodness.

You are good and ready to forgive, and plenteous in mercy unto all who call upon You.

Father, You are good to all who wait for You, to the soul who seeks You.

It is Your goodness, O Lord, that leads us to repentance.

Our righteousness is as filthy rags. May we see ourselves as You see us, so that we may come to You for pardon.

Father, we read of Jesus' temptation in the wilderness. The devil quotes Your Word to tempt Him. May we study the Bible daily so that, like Jesus, we may be able to say to the devil, "It is written again."

We pray, "Lead us not into temptation," for we know how weak we are. We ask You, Father, to deliver us from evil and we trust You to keep us from evil.

Honor Jesus' prayer, Father, when He prayed that You would not take us out of the world, but that You would keep us from evil.

Help us not to resist evil, but give us strength to depart from evil.

Help us to resist the devil and he will flee from us.

Ruler of all things, of all people, send Your angels to keep us and protect us from evil.

Give us fear of You, so that we may depart from evil.

Give us wisdom, so that we may not be ignorant of Satan's devices.

Lead us not into temptation, Father, but be with us every second of every minute of every hour of the day and night.

Strengthen us so that we will be able to resist temptations of body and mind.

We know the awfulness of sin and we know our weakness, Father, and we are afraid of the hours of testing. Be forever with us.

You instruct us, Father, to put off anger, wrath, malice, blasphemy, and filthy communication out of our mouth. You tell us: lie not one to another, seeing that we have put off the old man with his deeds, and have put on the new man, who is renewed in knowledge after the image of You, our Creator.

We know we have a terrible enemy and that he goes about as a roaring lion seeking whom he may devour. Deliver us from him, Father. Deliver us from the hosts of sin, which are pressing hard to draw us away from You.

Keep us from the hour of temptation, which shall come upon all of the world to try it.

Deliver us from a proud look, a lying tongue, and hands that shed innocent blood, from a heart that devises wicked imaginations, from feet that be swift in running to mischief, and from being a false witness who speaks lies. May we not sow discord among our brothers, for these things are an abomination to You, our Lord.

Deliver us from pride.

Deliver us from arrogance.

Deliver us from greed of gain.

Deliver us from class and race prejudice.

Deliver us from envy, which is the rottenness of the bones.

Deliver us from family strife.

Deliver us from hardness of heart.

Deliver us from apathy.

Deliver us from resentment.

Deliver us from suspicion.

Deliver us from jealousy.

Deliver us from depression.

Deliver us from fear of unemployment.

May we hate evil so that we may come to the light, Jesus, for You are the light of the world.

Search us, O God, and know our hearts: try us and know our thoughts and see if there be any wicked way in us, and lead us in the way everlasting. Lead us not into temptation, for we are very weak.

We understand, Father, that our temptations are common to man, and that You are faithful and will not suffer us to be tempted above what we are able to bear, but will with the temptation make a way to escape, so that we may be able to bear it. Help us to see the way of escape and take it. We pray for Your strength. Give us daily strength for daily needs.

Since the love of money is the root of all evil, take away our desire to be rich, which causes us to fall into temptation and a snare, and into many foolish and hurtful lusts which drown us in destruction and perdition.

Enable us to check all evil thoughts and passions.

Grant us the help of Your grace. Keep us from falling.

Open our eyes, turn us from darkness to light, from the power of Satan unto You.

Make us honest—otherwise we pray in vain.

May we confess our faults one to another and pray one for another.

We have neglected visiting our parents, our relatives, our friends. Forgive, Lord.

We forget all about You, Lord, and are indifferent to our neighbor. Forgive.

May we be quick to sympathize with those who are in trouble.

> Cast out our sins, and enter in,
> Be born in us today!
> O come to us, abide in us,
> Our Lord Immanuel.
> —Phillips Brooks

Take away our carnal minds and give us spiritual minds; for the carnal mind cannot be subject to Your law, O God, but to be spiritually minded is life and peace.

May we seek to give love, joy, and peace rather than to receive.

We know, Father, that goodness is not what we do, but what we are, and that we can have no more goodness of our own than we can have a life of our own. We can only be good as we partake of Your holiness.

May we follow the path of the just, which is as the shining light that shines more and more unto the perfect day.

65

Come, Holy Spirit, in all your power and might. Come in Your Own gentle way.

> Holy Father, great Creator,
> Source of mercy, love and peace,
> Look upon the Mediator,
> Clothe us with His righteousness.
> —Alexander Viets Griswold

> Breathe on us, Breath of God,
> Fill us with life anew,
> That we may love what You love
> And do what You would do.

> Breathe on us, Breath of God,
> Until our hearts are pure,
> Until with You we will one will,
> To do or to endure.
> —Edwin Hatch, alt.

Give us godliness, which is profitable unto all things, having promise of the life that now is, and that which is to come.

Thank You, Jesus, for giving Yourself for our sins, so that You might deliver us from this present evil world, according to the will of God, our Father.

Help us to keep Your commandments so we may not fear evil.

May we have no other gods before You.

May we worship only You, O God.

Help us to take not Your Name in vain, for You will not hold us guiltless if we do.

May we keep holy the Sabbath day.

Help us to honor our father and our mother so that our days may be long upon this land.

May we not steal, kill or commit adultery.

May we not bear false witness against our neighbor or covet anything that is our neighbor's.

May we bear one another's burdens and so fulfill the law of Christ.

Give us the power to control our tongues and our lips, so that they speak no evil.

Teach us that our pleas are in vain, Lord, unless we do the things that You say. We deceive ourselves if we are hearers of the Word only, and not doers.

Help us to do Your will; then You shall hear us when we pray.

Help us to keep Your commandments and to do those things that are pleasing in Your sight, and whatsoever we ask of You we shall receive.

Lord, revive Your Church, beginning with us.

Open our ears so that we may hear. Open our eyes so that we may see our opportunities to do good to all, for inasmuch as we do it not unto the least we do it not unto You.

Help us to loose the bands of wickedness, to undo the heavy burdens, to let the oppressed go free and to break every yoke.

May we deal our bread to the hungry and bring the poor who are cast out to our houses. May we feed the hungry, give drink to the thirsty, clothe the naked. Then shall we call and You will answer, we shall cry and You will say, Here I am.

May we defend the poor and orphans, do justice to the afflicted and needy. May we deliver the poor and needy, and rid them out of the hands of the wicked.

May we neglect not to visit the sick and those in prison.

May we ever be aware of our opportunities to do good unto all men, meeting their needs. Father, put us always in remembrance of these things. Though we know them, we seem not to remember them at the right time.

We read in the Bible that if we break one of the least commandments and teach men so, we shall be called the least in the kingdom of heaven, and that if we do Your commandments and teach them, we shall be called great in the kingdom of heaven. May we love Your commandments.

May we never forget that truth is forever truth and right is forever right.

Help us to be our best today.

Help us to do our best today.

Teach us so that we may serve You, Lord, even if with bent or broken tools.

Teach us that those who do Your work are those who believe in Jesus. We know, Father, that Your righteousness is available to all who believe.

Lord, we bless You because You have heard the voice of our supplications.

Lord, we bless You, for You have not turned away our prayers, or Your mercy from us.

You sent Your angel to deliver us.

We sought You, Lord, and You heard us, and delivered us from all our fears.

You, Lord, shall preserve us from all evil: You shall preserve our souls.

You shall preserve our going out and our coming in, from this time forth and even forevermore.

Help us to be rich in good works, ready to distribute, willing to communicate, so that we may lay hold on eternal life.

May we grow in grace and in the knowledge of our Lord and Savior, Jesus Christ!

May we glory only in You, O Lord, Who exercises judgment and righteousness in the earth, for in these things You delight.

May we show forth Your goodness not only with our lips, but in our lives.

Whenever we praise You, Father, we want our lips and lives to agree. When we profess Your Name, may our hearts confess Your love.

Fill us so full of Your goodness, Father, that a bit will splash out on every person we meet!

Lord,
teach us
kindness

A kind soul is a river of gladness.

May we be just and true; may we be kind to each other as You, Lord, are kind to us.

Fill us with Your kindness, Lord, for we cannot be just if we are not kindhearted.

Make us gentle, courteous and forbearing.

Give us sympathy with all who suffer wrong.

Help us to do to others as we wish they would do to us.

May we speak kind words, for then we shall hear kind echoes.

Remind us that a gentle word may soothe some heart and banish pain.

Any kindness, Lord, that we show is a simple expression of Your love.

May we not forget that the kindest thing we can do for ourselves is to be kind to others.

Make us eager to help.

We understand that kindness is deep, delicate love.

We seldom speak a kind word in vain.

Kindness is great wisdom.

Perfect us, Father; make us gentle and kind.

We feel so near to You, dear Lord, when we show kindness to one of Your children, and even nearer when we are kind to an enemy.

May we blot all unkindness from our memory.

How gentle are God's commands! How kind His precepts are!

May we increase the joy of life for all of our neighbors by small kindnesses.

Father, You shall feed Your flock like a shepherd; You shall gather the lambs with Your arm, and carry them in Your bosom, and shall gently lead those that are with young. Oh, lead us gently home, Father.

And may we learn to be gentle and kind to ourselves.

How excellent is Your loving-kindness, O God! Therefore the children of men put their trust under the shadow of Your wings.

> Jesus, gentlest Savior,
> God of might and power,
> You, Yourself, are dwelling
> With us at this hour.
> —Frederick William Faber, alt.

> O, hope of every contrite heart!
> O, joy of all the meek!
> To those who fall, how kind You are!
> How good to those who seek.
> —Bernard of Clairvaux

May we be kind one to another, tenderhearted, forgiving one another, even as You, Father, for Christ's sake have forgiven us.

O God, help us to heal the broken in heart and bind up their wounds.

Help us to be friendly and thoughtful to others.

Even when we were friendly, we were not friendly enough. We could have been more friendly. Forgive.

When we have been offended, we have counted the offender as an enemy and not as a brother to be admonished. Forgive.

May we be careful not to say unkind words, and let us not be unkind in silence.

May we learn to use kind words in abundance.

Help us to show forth Your loving-kindness in the morning and Your faithfulness every night.

May we always speak gently and let no harsh words mar any good we may do.

Help us to be especially kind to those who spend so much of their lives with us.

Help us to remember kindnesses shown to us as easily as we recall the offenses.

Father, we would now give thanks to You for Your marvelous kindness to us and to all men.

We thank You that though our outward man perish, You renew our inward man day by day.

Thank You for being kind to the thankful and the unthankful.

Thank You for sending the rain on the just and the unjust.

Thank You for bearing our burdens.

Thank You for the yoke of Jesus, which is easy, and His burden, which is light.

Thank You for our prayers that You have not answered, or rather that You answered with a "No."

Thank You for those who are kind to us.

Help us, Jesus, to do our Father's will, like You—to share our neighbor's grief.

May we always give kind looks, kind words and kind acts.

May we learn to give to everyone who asks of us.

May we do all we can to make life less difficult for those who live around us.

As we grow in age, may we grow in grace and kindliness.

So teach us to number our days that we may apply our hearts unto wisdom.

Give us wisdom so that we may win souls.

May we always stop to be kind, though we often swerve from our path.

You have shown such kindly judgment to our failings, Lord!

Lord,
teach us
meekness

Those who know God are humble.

Humility leads us to God.

Humility is the cornerstone of all the virtues.

Our virtue can be measured by the degree of our humility.

One plants, one waters, but God gives the increase.

Father to Whom we address our prayers, You are the very Lord of the universe. You are indeed King of kings and Lord of lords. You are the author of all things by the word of Your power and might. To You belong all might, majesty, dominion and power.

You have made the earth by Your power, You have established the world by Your wisdom, and have stretched out the heavens by Your understanding.

You are great, O Lord, and of great power. Your understanding is infinite.

You, Lord, in the beginning laid the foundations of the earth, and the heavens are the work of Your hands.

By Your word, O Lord, were the heavens made, and all the host of them by the breath of Your mouth.

Lord, You are God, Who made heaven and earth and the sea and all that is in them.

By Your strength You set fast the mountains, being girded with power.

> We think of You, O God, the Mighty Source
> Of all things; the stupendous force
> On which all strength depends;
> From Whose mighty arms, beneath Whose eyes,
> All period, power, and enterprise
> Commences, reigns, and ends.
> —Christopher Smart, alt.

O God, You rule by Your power forever. Your eyes behold the nations.

79

You still the noise of the seas, the noise of the waves and the tumult of the people.

You cause the vapors to ascend from the ends of the earth; You make lightning for the rain; You bring the wind out of Your treasuries.

You tell the number of the stars; You call them all by name.

You give food to all flesh.

You form the light and create darkness; You make peace, and create evil; You, the Lord, do all of these things.

O everlasting God, the Lord, the Creator of the ends of the earth, You faint not and are not weary. There is no searching of Your understanding. You give power to the faint and for those who have no might You increase their strength.

God of all flesh, there is nothing too hard for You.

> Father, from You all skill and science flow,
> All pity, care and love,
> All calm and courage, faith and hope—
> O pour them from above!
> —Charles Kingsley

You are a God at hand and a God far off. None can hide in a secret place so that You shall not see him. You fill heaven and earth!

Father, we know You can do everything, and that no thought can be withheld from You.

May we give You the glory due unto Your Name!

O Lord, how great are Your works!

May the people praise You, O God, may all the people praise You. Then shall the earth yield her increase; and You, our own God, shall bless us; and all the ends of the earth shall fear You.

Unto You, Father, we lift up our eyes. You dwell in the heavens; with You is the fountain of life. In Your light shall we see light.

Our help is in the Name of the Lord, Who made heaven and earth.

Riches and honor come of You, and You reign over all; in Your hand is power and might; in Your hand it is to make great, and to give strength unto all. Now therefore, our God, we thank You and praise Your glorious Name!

> We have no help but Thine, O God, nor do we need
> Another arm save Yours to lean upon;
> It is enough, our Lord, enough indeed:
> Our strength is in Your might—Your might alone.
> —Horatius Bonar, alt.

Though You be high, O Lord, yet You have respect unto the lowly.

Jesus, may we take Your yoke upon us, and learn of You; for You are meek and lowly in heart, and we shall find rest unto our souls.

Jesus humbled Himself even unto His death on the cross. May we humble ourselves in Your sight, O Lord, and You will lift us up.

Show us Your purpose for our lives.

Help us to deny ourselves, to take up our cross daily and follow You.

Teach us that submission to You heals all wounds.

And if a man be overtaken in a fault, may we restore such a one in the spirit of meekness, considering ourselves lest we also be tempted.

May we bear the infirmity of our weak brother rather than act to please ourselves.

Hide Your face from our sins and blot out all of our iniquities.

For Your Name's sake, O Lord, pardon our iniquity, for it is great.

May we pardon so that You may pardon us.

May we never forget that there is no Name under heaven given to man in Whom and through Whom we may receive salvation, other than Your Son, Jesus.

We know there is one God, and one mediator between God and us: the man Christ Jesus, Who gave Himself as a ransom for all.

Christ is able to save to the uttermost all who come unto You through Him, Father, as He ever lives to make intercession for us.

Strip us of ourselves and give us Yourself.

May we seek You, Lord, and Your strength; may we seek Your face evermore.

As we seek You, Lord, we rejoice and are glad in You. May such as love Your salvation say, "The Lord be magnified!"

May we remember that the fewer words the better prayer, for we are not heard for our much speaking. Let not our tongue out-run our heart as we pray.

We know that we have this treasure in earthen vessels so that the excellency of the power may be of You, Lord, and not of us.

May we be strong in You and in the power of Your might.

> Our thoughts, before they are our own,
> Are to You, O God, distinctly known.
> You know the words we mean to speak,
> Ere from our opening lips they break.
> —Isaac Watts, alt.

Oh, help us, Jesus, in meekness to instruct those who oppose themselves, so that You may give them repentance to the ac-knowledging of the truth and so that they may recover them-selves out of the snare of the devil.

May we submit ourselves to every ordinance of man for the Lord's sake; for so is Your will, O God.

May we render to Caesar the things that are Caesar's and to You the things that are Yours.

May we make prayers and intercessions, and give thanks for those in authority.

May we do nothing through strife or vainglory; but in lowliness of mind let each esteem others better than ourselves.

May we be silent so that our hearts may listen for Your voice.

Keep us mindful of the fact that we brought nothing into this world, and it is certain that we shall carry nothing out.

May we not forget that we are appointed once to die, and after that the judgment.

May we never boast of tomorrow, for we know not what a day may bring forth. Let us say that if the Lord wills it, we shall do this or that.

May we never love the praise of men more than the praise of God.

May we be subject unto the higher power, for there is no power but of You, our God: the powers that be are ordained of You. If we resist the power, we resist Your ordinance, and if we resist we shall receive to ourselves damnation. Help us to pay tribute also, for they are Your ministers.

May Your Spirit direct and rule our hearts in all things, at all times.

Teach us that we do not live by bread alone, but by every word that proceeds out of Your mouth.

If we think we stand, may we take heed lest we fall.

Help us to cast out the beam in our own eye so that we may see clearly to cast the mote out of our brother's eye.

Give us the mind of Christ.

Keep us humble, Lord, for You give grace unto the lowly.

For the hearts of children
Hold what worlds cannot,
And the God of wonders
Loves the lowly spot.
—Frederick William Faber, alt.

May we always remember that the angels of the little children do behold Your face, O Father.

Give us humble, lowly, contrite hearts,
Believing, true and clean;
Which neither life nor death can part
From You, Lord, Who dwells within.
—Charles Wesley, alt.

Keep us ever in the simplicity that is in Christ.

Lord,
teach us temperance

He who cannot command himself is not free.

He who is master of himself is great.

Conquer self.

If the Son makes us free, we are free indeed!

May we offend not in word, for if we learn this, we are able also to bridle the whole body.

Although our tongue is a little member, it boasts of great things and we know how great an amount a little fire kindles.

We know we cannot tame our tongue without Your help, Father, for which we plead. Our tongue is an unruly evil, full of deadly poison.

Our tongue is a fire, a world of iniquity; it defiles our whole body and is set on fire of hell. Lord, help!

May we sin not by proud speech.

May we soon learn that it is not what goes into our mouths that defiles us, but that which comes out of our mouths.

May we not speak evil of another.

May we order our conversation aright; then shall we see Your salvation, O Father.

You keep a guard on our lips, dear Lord.

Set a watch, O Lord, before our mouths; keep the door of our lips.

May we exercise self-control, which will enable us to think or say nothing which may injure our neighbors or ourselves.

And, O Jesus, may we never deny You before men, for if we do, You will deny us before our Father in heaven.

Give us the grace to confess You before men: then You will confess us before our Father in heaven.

Freely we have received. Help us to freely give in the Name of Jesus, Who gave His life for us.

Help us to speak of the glory of Your kingdom.

Help us to glorify You in our body and in our spirit, which are Yours, for we are bought with a price.

We praise You, Lord, for we are fearfully and wonderfully made.

Imbue us daily with the competency of Your wisdom, so that we may be able to further glorify Your holy Name.

May we walk worthy of You, our God, Who has called us into Your kingdom.

Consecrate our speech to Your service.

Let no corrupt communication proceed out of our mouths, but only that which instructs and improves.

Help us to be masters of ourselves, so that we may be servants of Yours.

Today give us self-control in speech and temper.

Let the words of our mouths, and the meditations of our hearts, be acceptable in Your sight, O Lord, our Strength and our Redeemer.

Lord,
teach us
faith

All the scholastic scaffolding tumbles down before the word "faith."

Faith is to believe what we do not see. Faith's reward is to see and enjoy what we believe.

What we are depends very much on what we believe.

The most useful knowledge requires the largest faith.

Father, You have dealt to every man the measure of faith, and we thank You for this precious gift.

We know, Father, that without faith it is impossible to please You; for he who comes to You must believe that You are and that You are a rewarder of those who diligently seek You.

May we diligently seek You through the study of Your Word, for faith comes by hearing, and hearing by Your Word.

May we take unto us Your whole armor, so that we may be able to withstand in the evil day. We need Your truth and righteousness, Your gospel of peace, Your Word and, above all, faith, wherewith we shall be able to quench all the fiery darts of the wicked.

This is the victory that overcomes the world—our faith, which is Your gift to us, Father.

Day by day, guide us to see You in Your Word.

It is through faith that we understand that the worlds were framed by Your Word; that in the beginning You created the heavens and the earth. You said, "Let there be light," and there was light!

Through faith we understand that You, Father, formed man of the dust of the ground and breathed into his nostrils the breath of life so that man became a living soul, and that You caused Adam to sleep and from one of his ribs made a woman.

Show us great and mighty things that we know not.

God of hope, fill us with all joy and peace in believing, that we may abound in hope, through the power of the Holy Spirit.

Knowing that we cannot be justified by works, give us the faith of Jesus so that we may be justified.

May we meditate on Your Word daily, for the holy scriptures are able to make us wise unto salvation through faith in Jesus Christ.

The prophet declared: "The Lord Himself shall give you a sign; Behold, a virgin shall conceive, and bear a son, and shall call His Name Immanuel."

We also read: "But thou, Bethlehem of Ephratah, though thou be little among the thousands of Judah, yet out of thee shall come forth unto Me that is to be ruler in Israel; Whose goings forth have been from of old, from everlasting." We believe this report, Father.

As the prophet foretold: Your Son was despised and rejected of men; a man of sorrows, and acquainted with grief, and we hid our faces from Him; He was despised, and we esteemed Him not. Surely He has borne our griefs, and carried our sorrows: yet we did esteem Him stricken, smitten of God, and afflicted. But He was wounded for our transgressions, He was bruised for our iniquities, the chastisement of our peace was upon Him; and with His stripes we are healed.

All we like sheep have gone astray; we have turned every one to his own way; and You, Father, have laid on Jesus the iniquity of us all. He was oppressed, and He was afflicted, yet He opened not His mouth: It pleased You, Father, to bruise Him, to put Him to grief that we might be saved.

May we not stray from You, Jesus, for You are the way.

May we not doubt You, Jesus, for You are the truth.

Teach us to trust You.

Jesus! only Name that's given
Under all the mighty heaven,
Whereby man, to sin enslaved
Bursts his fetters and is saved.
　　—William Walsham How

Jesus, You are the way, to You alone
From sin and death we flee;
For he who would the Father seek,
Must seek Him, Lord, by Thee.
　　　　—George W. Doane, alt.

We understand that there is but one God, the Father, of Whom are all things, and we in Him; and one Lord, Jesus Christ, by Whom are all things, and we by Him; and there is one Spirit.

We are the children of God by faith in Christ Jesus. There is neither Jew nor Greek, there is neither bond nor free, there is neither male nor female: for we are all one in Christ Jesus.

Thank You, Father, for giving us Your Spirit to bear witness with our spirit that we are Your children, and if children, then heirs. We are heirs of God and joint heirs with Christ, if we suffer with Him so that we might be also glorified with Him.

You, O God, have chosen the poor of this world, rich in faith, as heirs of the kingdom which You have promised to those who love You.

Jesus, You shall reign where e'er the sun
Does its successive journeys run,
Your kingdom spread from shore to shore,
Till moons shall wax and wane no more.
　　　　　—Isaac Watts, alt.

For unto us a child is born, unto us a son is given: and the government shall be upon His shoulder; and His Name shall be called Wonderful, Counselor, the Mighty God, the Everlasting Father, the Prince of Peace. Of the increase of His government and peace there shall be no end, upon the throne of David and upon His kingdom, to order it, and to establish it from henceforth, even forever. The zeal of the Lord of hosts shall perform this.

Oh, for a world at unity with itself. May all nations soon bring their glory and honor into Your kingdom, O Christ.

You are our God forever and ever. You will be our guide even unto death.

Give us grace to follow day by day in the steps of Jesus.

Show us Your ways, O Lord; teach us Your paths. Lead us in Your truth.

May we daily search the scriptures, for in them we think we have eternal life.

Give us strength so that we may earnestly contend for the faith that was once delivered unto the saints.

Lord of all faith, the gospel of Christ is the power of God unto salvation to everyone who believes. Neither is there salvation in any other: for there is no other Name under heaven given among men whereby we may be saved.

In Christ dwells all the fullness of the Godhead bodily, and we are complete in Him, Who is the head of all principality and power.

If we believe that Jesus is the Christ, we are born of God.

If we are born again we overcome the world, and the victory that overcomes the world is our faith.

Other foundation can no man lay than that which is laid, which is Jesus Christ.

We know, Father, that we are saved through faith, which is not of ourselves, but a gift from You; we are saved not through works, lest we should boast.

Jesus, You are the living bread that came down from heaven: if any man eats of this bread, he shall live forever. Give us this bread.

Jesus, You are the door, and if we enter by this door, You, we shall be saved.

You, Jesus, are the stone that the builders rejected, and You have become the head of the corner. If we fall on this stone, we shall be broken, but if it falls on us, it will grind us to powder. Mercy, Lord!

Help us to confess with our mouth Jesus, our Lord, and to believe in our heart that He is raised from the dead. So shall we be saved, for with the heart man believes unto righteousness, and with the mouth confession is made unto salvation.

If we believe in the Son we have everlasting life; if we do not believe in the Son we shall not see life, but the wrath of God shall be upon us.

We walk by faith, not by sight. The just shall live by faith.

May we ever take the shield of faith, which is able to quench all the fiery darts of the wicked.

The end of our faith is the salvation of our souls.

Jesus Christ is the same yesterday, today and forever.

Though You slay us, yet will we trust You.

The things that are impossible with men are possible with You, our God.

Thank You for Your abiding presence, for Your strength which is always sufficient. When troubled on every side, we are not distressed; we may be perplexed, but not in despair; persecuted, but not forsaken; cast down, but not destroyed.

Thank You for the faith that with You nothing shall be impossible.

Help us to abide in You. Abide in us; call to our mind Your holy words.

> Open our ears that we may hear
> Voices of truth You send so clear.
> —C. H. Scott, alt.

Water of life, give us the water that shall be in us a well of water springing up into everlasting life.

May we never forget that what You have promised You are able to perform.

Give us faith to believe that we shall receive when we ask.

May we not cast away our confidence, for our reward for believing will be great.

> Let faith each weak petition fill,
> And waft it to the skies,
> And teach our hearts 'tis Goodness still
> That grants it, or denies.
> —Joseph Dacre Carlyle

May we continue in the faith, grounded and settled, and be not moved away from the hope of You, our God.

May we ever ask, may we ever seek, may we ever knock: for everyone who asks receives, he who seeks finds and to him who knocks it shall be opened.

May we always be willing to place ourselves with perfect trust into Your loving hands.

Heal us, O Lord, and we shall be healed. Save us and we shall be saved, for You are our praise.

Let us call for the elders of the Church, and let them pray over our sick, anointing them with oil in Your Name. And their prayer of faith shall save the sick, and You, Lord, shall raise them up; and if they have committed sins, they shall be forgiven them.

May we trust in Your power to heal.

Help us, Lord, to confess our faults one to another, to pray one for another, so that we may be healed.

Father, we know that the effectual, fervent prayer of a righteous man avails much.

You even hear our prayers without words.

Let us not stagger at Your promises through unbelief.

This is the confidence that we have in You, Father, that if we ask anything according to Your will, You hear us; and if we know that You hear us, whatsoever we ask, we know that we have the petition that we desire of You.

We know that if two of us shall agree on earth concerning anything that we shall ask, it shall be done for us of You, our Father, Who is in heaven.

We believe that when two or three are gathered together in Jesus' Name, You, our Lord, are there in the midst.

We have trusted in Your mercy, and we shall rejoice in Your salvation.

We give glory to You for healing our bodies.

You, Lord, are our rock, and our fortress, and our deliverer; our God, our strength in Whom we will trust; our buckler, and the horn of our salvation and our high tower.

May we ever trust in You and never lean on our own understanding.

May we cast all our care upon You, for You care for us.

Give us Your joy, which is the result of trust, when we find no joy around us.

We can now see that all that we have needed has been granted in what You, our loving heavenly Father, ordained for us.

We are fellow citizens with the saints, and of the household of God, and are built upon the foundation of the apostles and prophets, Jesus Christ Himself being the chief cornerstone; in Him all of the building, fitly framed together, grows unto a holy temple in the Lord; in Him we are built together for a place of abode of the Spirit. Praise God.

May the grace of our Lord Jesus Christ, and the love of God, and the communion of the Holy Spirit be with us all.

May we daily increase in the Holy Spirit more and more. We want more love, more peace, more patience, more joy, more faith, more kindness each day until we see You face to face.

Help us to add virtue to our faith; and to virtue, knowledge; and to knowledge, temperance; and to temperance, patience; and to patience, godliness; and to godliness, charity; for if these things be in us, and abound, we shall be fruitful in the knowledge of our Lord, Jesus Christ.

Even so—
Come, Lord Jesus

Thine, O Lord, is the greatness, and the power, and the glory, and the victory, and the majesty: for all that is in the heaven and in the earth is Thine; Thine is the kingdom, O Lord, and Thou art exalted as head above all.

All power is given unto You, Jesus, in heaven and in earth.

Jesus, You are far above all principality, and power, and might, and dominion, and every name that is named—not only in this world, but also in that which is to come.

Let every tongue confess with one accord in heaven and in earth that Jesus Christ is Lord.

Glory be to Jesus, Who has gone to prepare a place for us in our Father's house.

Holy, Holy, Holy, Lord God Almighty, which was, and is, and is to come.

Your kingdom come. Jesus said, "My kingdom is not of this world."

Your kingdom, which is not in word, but in power—come.

Your kingdom, which is like a merchant seeking goodly pearls, who, when he found one of great price, sold all that he had and bought it—come.

Your kingdom, which is like a grain of mustard seed, which a man took, and cast into his garden; and it grew, and waxed a great tree; and the fowls of the air lodged in the branches thereof—come.

Your kingdom, which is like leaven, which a woman took, and hid in three measures of meal, till the whole was leavened—come.

Teach us, Lord, that Your kingdom comes not with observation: Your kingdom is within us!

May we be born again so that we may see the kingdom of God.

May we be born of water and of the Spirit, that we may enter into the kingdom of God.

Make us poor in spirit, Lord: then ours is the kingdom of heaven.

May we be converted and become as little children, so that we may enter into the kingdom of heaven.

May we never forget the little children, for of such is the kingdom of God.

The kingdom, the dominion and the greatness of the kingdom under the whole heaven, shall be given to the saints of the Most High, Whose kingdom is an everlasting kingdom, and all dominions shall serve You, O God.

You, Lord, have prepared Your throne in the heavens, and Your kingdom rules over all.

Your kingdom is an everlasting kingdom, and Your dominion endures throughout all generations.

Your kingdom come in our hearts, O Lord. Rule our lives completely.

Your kingdom is coming, dear Lord. May we have a share in bringing in the kingdom. Be watching and waiting, that sight to behold!

You, Lord, the righteous judge, will give a crown of righteousness unto all of those who love Your appearing.

We look toward that day of Christ's coming when He shall have delivered up the kingdom to You, Father, when He shall have put down all rule and all authority and power. For Jesus must reign until He has put all enemies under His feet, including the last enemy, which is death.

The glory to come will far outweigh the sufferings we now endure. All creation is moving on to redemption through the mystery of pain. Our hope is sure and we wait with patience for You, though we groan within ourselves.

Lord, keep us humble, for that day will come when the lofty looks of man shall be humbled and the haughtiness of man shall be bowed down, and the Lord alone shall be exalted in that day.

O God, You have highly exalted Jesus and have given Him a Name which is above every name, so that at the Name of Jesus every knee should bow, of things in heaven, and things in earth, and things under the earth, and that every tongue should confess that Jesus Christ is Lord, to the glory of You, our Father.

It is but a little while and Christ shall come again. He died so that we may live and He lives so that we may reign with Him.

We shall see the Son of man coming in a cloud with power and great glory.

> Lo, He comes with clouds descending,
> Once for our salvation slain;
> Thousand angel-hosts attending
> Swell the triumph of His train.
> Christ, the Lord returns to reign.
> —Charles Wesley, alt.

When Christ, Who is our life, shall appear, then shall we also appear with Him in glory.

O Lord, we want to be in that number when the saints go marchin' in.

Father, may we watch and be ready for that day when Jesus shall come with his angels and we shall receive our reward.

Help us to remember that we shall give account of ourselves to God. You will bring every work into judgment, with every secret thing, whether it be good, or whether it be evil.

Help us to be always ready, for You, Jesus, will come at an hour when we think not.

We commit ourselves unto You, knowing You are able to keep us. You, Lord, shall deliver us from every evil work, and shall preserve us unto Your heavenly kingdom: We give You glory forever and ever.

Help us to spread this gospel of the kingdom in all the world, for a witness unto all nations; then shall Your kingdom come.

We thank You, Jesus, for preparing us a place, and that You will come for us so that we will be where You are and we will be like You, for we will see You as You are! Only when we see You as You are will we praise You as we ought.

Behold! You, Jesus, stand at the door and knock. If any man hears Your voice and opens the door, You will come to him and will sup with him, and he with You. And to he who overcomes You will grant to sit with You in Your throne, even as You overcame, and are set down with our Father in His throne.

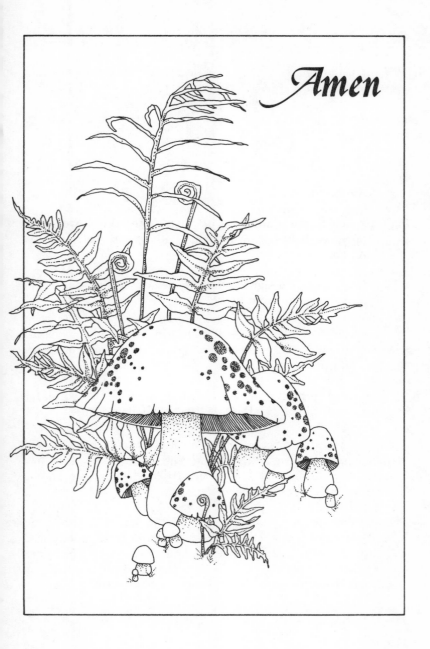

Amen

Amen—so be it.

Amen is the affirmation of inner faith. When we pray, we believe You hear us, Father, and we say Amen.

Our Amen is a sign of sincerity—evidence that our prayers are from our heart.

As our Amen is sincere, so is our prayer.